KOREAN WAR

A History From Beginning to End

Copyright © 2016 by Hourly History Limited

Table of Contents

Introduction

The Korean War began in 1950 when North Korea invaded South Korea in an attempt to reunite the two halves of the peninsula under one communist government. It was not a civil war, and neither was it simply a war to gain more land, since the two sides shared a common past, and in some ways, a common identity.

The Korean War lasted just over three years, from June 1950 through July 1953, but it was one of the most important early events of the Cold War. This conflict, between the United States and the Soviet Union, encompassed the entire world in an ideological battle between two opposing economic systems – communism and capitalism – and their accompanying cultures and ways of life.

The United States and the Soviet Union involved themselves directly or indirectly in every conflict between their two respective economic systems. Therefore, the Korean War was not just a battle over sovereignty of the Korean Peninsula. Events in this small corner of the globe thus reverberated widely; for three years, the eyes of the world were on Korea. Within months, it would involve the United Nations, the United States, China, and the Soviet Union. Events on the small peninsula bordering China threatened to plunge the world back into another world war.

By the time the war ended, nothing - and everything - had changed. The imaginary line dividing North and

South Korea remained in the same place. However, the fates of Koreans were forever altered, and the course of the Cold War would not be the same again either.

Chapter One

Korea before World War II

"Even if you know the way, ask again."

—Korean Proverb

Today, we know Korea as two distinct places: communist North Korea, run by a controversial dictator, and "free" South Korea, a small, supposedly heavily urban country focused on technology and industry. However, it was not until 1945 that Korea was split into two separate states run by two separate governments. Korea has a long history before that time.

Korea is a peninsula. It shares its northern border with China and is surrounded on all other sides by sea: The Yellow Sea on the west and the Sea of Japan on the east. Southern Japan is located off of Korea's south-eastern coast.

During its early history (as early as the 1st or 2nd centuries CE), three separate kingdoms existed on the Korean Peninsula. As the centuries wore on, these three kingdoms warred with each other more and more. Eventually, the kingdoms were united, though continued warfare and changes in power, combined with spotty survival of records, make this early history of Korea difficult. One of the three Korean kingdoms was called

Goguryeo—later Goryeo – and provides us the etymological root of the name "Korea."

It was not only the Three Kingdoms that initiated warfare and caused instability on the Korean peninsula during its early history. China, too, wished to control Korea. Several Chinese rulers from a number of dynasties launched warfare in Korea, including the Mongol Dynasty, which eventually conquered the peninsula in the 13th century.

In consideration of Korea's very long history, Mongol rule did not last very long. By the end of the 14th century, the Mongols had collapsed, and despite ensuing instability in Korea, the Kingdom of Joseon was established by the military leader Yi Seonggye. This kingdom existed for more than five hundred years.

Europeans began trading in Asia and the Far East, via the overland Silk Road spice routes, while much of this turbulence with China was going on. However, European colonization of Korea would not begin until later. By the nineteenth century, when Europeans were looking to extend their eastern empires beyond India, Korea had a reputation for being isolationist. This was largely in response to repeated attempts, particularly by the Chinese, to overtake it. As a result, Korea had earned the nickname the "Hermit Kingdom."

Japan was also traditionally isolationist. The allegory goes that American Navy Commodore Matthew Perry sailed to Japan and demanded she open herself to trade, and she complied. In reality, the arrival of Commodore Perry was just the last in a series of events that prompted

Japan to open its ports to foreign trade and to modernize in order to prevent conquest.

Korea did not read these signs the same way, at least not initially. True to their nickname, they remained closed off to the rest of the world until early in the twentieth century. At that point, they finally decided to attempt to modernize, but it was too late. In 1910, fresh from their 1905 victory over Russia in the Russo-Japanese War, Japan conquered Korea with little trouble. Like many European countries had been doing for hundreds of years, Japan was also working on building an empire. While European conquest was usually tolerated and even celebrated, this was not the case with Japan: much racism existed against the Japanese (as with all Asians). In the years during and surrounding World War II this would be a serious issue; for Korea, it would impact the post-war world and the causes of the Korean War.

Japanese rule was anything but peaceful. Despite western racism against them, they were also racist against other Asians, including Koreans. Japan saw Korea as an inferior nation of inferior people. Millions of Koreans were forced to labor to benefit Japan in virtual slavery; hundreds of thousands of women and very young girls were forced to become sex slaves for the Japanese (especially the military); tens of thousands of men and boys were forced to serve in the Japanese military, often in the most dangerous positions. Finally, more than four hundred thousand Koreans (at least) were killed as a direct result of the Japanese occupation.

By 1945, when World War II ended, Korea and Koreans had faced decades—even centuries—of hardship, discrimination, and violence. They were ready for peace. However, the end of the war would not set them up for this; in less than a decade, the tiny peninsula would once again be embroiled in war.

Chapter Two

The End of World War II and the Cold War Context

"No faction is better or worse than any other. All come from the same mold; they are all products of capitalist influence in the working class movement. And they are a poison that destroys our Party and the working class movement in Korea."

—Kim Jong-Il

The end of World War II brought both relief and uncertainty to Korea. On the one hand, the decades of suffering under Japan were over. The allies demanded unconditional surrender from Japan, and immediately went about disassembling its empire.

On the other hand, though, what this new peace would look like was not clear. Partially out of fear of instability, partially because of their own selfish interests, and partially because of racism, the Allies did not want to grant independence to the far-flung territories of the conquered nations.

This is not to say that Korea did not try. In August through September 1945, Koreans formed the People's Republic of Korea. This was a turbulent time, as the U.S. and the Soviet Union were working on securing the peninsula by ousting the last vestiges of the Japanese military and attempting to agree on how the peninsula would be governed. Despite their desire to establish home-rule, the United States Army Military Government in Korea (USAMGIK) rejected the new government formed by Koreans, in part because they suspected that it harbored communist sympathies.

While the Cold War divided the United States and the Soviet Union, they were both allies in World War II. Neither trusted the other, though, and deep suspicions existed between them, overshadowing the peace process. It was mostly because of this rivalry that control of Korea was divided along the now infamous 38th parallel (the line of latitude that runs 38 degrees north of the equator). The United States "administered" (simply put, controlled) the territory south of this line while the Soviet Union "administered" north of it. Two separate governments were established, and the two halves of Korea acted as states independent from one another.

This division did not result in peace, however: turbulent conflict would continue to rock Korea until the outbreak of war five years later. Much of this conflict centered on labor. A massive civil revolt called the Autumn Uprising took place in 1946. As a result, the United States declared martial law. Recognizing the futility of outwardly controlling Korea, they called on the United Nations to oversee the election of an independent Korean government. While this may seem realistic and perhaps even altruistic, in reality, the United States intended to operate a puppet regime by ensuring that a government friendly to their interests was elected. Even though the United States withdrew from Korea by the end of 1949, they remained involved, at least from a distance.

South Korea elected Rhee Syngman as their first president of the Republic of Korea. He is a controversial historical figure: While he advocated for Korean independence from the end of World War II, he also maintained tight control, was militantly anti-communist, and was at times responsible for brutal actions.

Meanwhile, recognizing the unfriendly environment in which they found themselves, communists and communist sympathizers fled South Korea, heading north. The Soviet Union also established a supposedly independent puppet government in North Korea, called the Democratic People's Republic of Korea, with Kim Il-sung (father of Kim Jong-Il and grandfather of present-day North Korean supreme leader Kim Jong-Un) as its leader. They withdrew in 1948, though like the United States, remained involved in North Korean affairs.

Atrocities in South Korea escalated tensions between communists and their opponents, as well as with North Korea. The Jeju uprising, a supposed communist revolt on Jeju Island off the southern coast of Korea, met with fierce repression; around 30,000 suspected communists were killed, and another 40,000 terrified residents fled (most of them to Japan).[1]

Violence also proliferated on the peninsula. By the outbreak of the Korean War in 1950, approximately 30,000 suspected communists had been put to death by the Rhee Syngman regime. Instances of sporadic violence were frequently blamed on communist activity in South Korea and were almost always met with brutal retaliation.

Events outside of Korea also played a role in the coming of the Korean War. As previously stated, the Korean War was a Cold War event, and the Cold War provided the global context for this conflict. One fact that made the tensions surrounding the Korean War worse was recent events in neighboring China. In 1949, much to the dismay of the United States and the pleasure of the Soviet Union, China fell to communism; at least initially, China was allied with the Soviet Union.

In the years immediately following World War II, the United States recognized communism as a serious, dangerous threat. Surrounding this belief, two important policies developed. The first was the Domino Theory. This theory stated that if one country fell to communism, others would soon follow, because the principles of communism would spread from country to country, and because communism needed allies in order to survive (a belief which has been disproven by history).

The policy of Containment followed the Domino Theory. If the Domino Theory was to be believed, then communism absolutely needed to be contained where it existed and not be allowed to spread at all. Therefore, the United States and its allies put many policies into practice that aimed to contain communism, including the Marshall Plan (to aid in rebuilding Europe) and the Truman Doctrine.

Containment is important to this story because the invasion of South Korea by communist North Korea was of much greater importance to the U.S. than just losing a relatively small ally. China, right next door, had just fallen. Both Korea and China were nearby to the Soviet Union. South Korea was the next in what the west perceived as a long line of countries that would fall to communism. Therefore, rolling back the North Koreans and protecting South Korea was of paramount importance. Communist North Korea was enough of a threat, but the United States could not allow South Korea to fall as well.

Further adding to U.S. suspicions that the Domino Theory was playing out were China's actions in Korea. During the Korean War, China would play a role, providing support (and more) to North Korea. By 1950, less than a year after China's fall to communism and the withdrawal of U.S. troops from South Korea, the conditions for another war were at hand.

Chapter Three

The Korean War Begins

"When I was six, the Korean War broke out, and all the classrooms were destroyed by war. We studied under the trees or in whatever buildings were left."

—Ban Ki-moon, South Korean politician

The Korean War between the communist north and capitalist south broke out in 1950. However, the south had been fighting this battle well before that date. Throughout the period after independence, South Korea had been hunting communists. Sometimes this turned violent, as discussed in the last chapter. Certainly, tensions between the two were very high by 1950.

South Korean leadership was not paranoid during these years. North Korean guerrillas *were* trying to infiltrate South Korea in order to prepare for a general invasion. By 1949, despite the very brutal and public deaths of suspected communists in South Korea, Kim Il-sung believed that his forces had made significant enough inroads to launch that invasion. However, wishing a swift, unconditional victory, he did not want to act alone. He first traveled to the Soviet Union to meet with Josef Stalin and try to persuade him to assist his invasion.

Stalin was not convinced, though within a year, his mind would change. Between 1949 and 1950, Americans withdrew their troops from Korea. China's communist takeover was much more complete and secure. Also, the Soviet Union felt that they had gained the upper hand (or at least equal footing) in the Cold War with the United States by designing and testing their own nuclear bomb and by breaking U.S. spy codes.

Therefore, by 1950, Stalin began to prepare North Korea for war as secretly as possible. He began quietly sending arms, taking the time to do so to avoid attracting attention from the United States. He also began sending the North Korean government more financial support, which was more overt. They also began training the North Korean armed forces and even sent troop units from the Chinese Revolution to North Korea as well. By April, both Stalin and Kim felt that North Korea was ready to invade. Mao Zedong, the leader of China, also agreed to assist North Korea if the need arose (Stalin knew that the Soviet Union itself could not intervene, lest they provoke the United States and initiate nuclear war).

Kim Il-sung did not want the world to perceive his actions as aggressive, or that he was merely trying to take over another sovereign region. Instead, he said he intended to reunite the country of Korea, which should not be divided into two separate entities. He thus held peninsula-wide elections in June, though very few people in South Korea were actually able to vote, which somewhat negated the purpose of the elections.

Then, Kim Il-sung sent a "peace" envoy to South Korean President Rhee Syngman to attempt to convince him to reunite the peninsula under communist rule. As would be expected, he rejected this proposal. It should be noted, however, that this was not because South Koreans did not want to reunite: in large part, they did, but not under communism.

South Korea was not innocent in the lead-up to the war, either. Fighting had been occurring periodically along the 38th parallel while all of these other events were unfolding in the spring and early summer of 1950, many of which were provoked by South Korea. South Korean military and political leaders also boasted about their military prowess, especially in comparison with the North Koreans. This did not help the escalating tensions.

Despite the rising tensions and serious preparations on the part of North Korea for war, South Korea remained largely oblivious and unsuspicious of the impending conflict. Even the United States Central Intelligence Agency did not pick up on it, even though they actively spied on North Korea.

War officially began on June 25, 1950, on the Ongjin Peninsula. This peninsula juts off of the western side of North Korea into the Yellow Sea. The Korean People's Army attacked, though claimed that they had only retaliated against an attack from the Army of the Republic of Korea, though it is unclear whether this was the case or not.

If the story told by the Korean People's Army was to be believed, it was not a smart move on the part of the South Koreans, as they were unprepared for war. Their army, particularly their heavy artillery, was seriously wanting. The number of trained members of the military was also very low in comparison with the North Koreans. However, as previously stated, South Korea and their allies, including the United States, remained ill-informed as to how much military build-up the North Koreans had done.

Almost immediately, fighting ensued all across the 38th parallel. With superior equipment and obviously better preparation, North Korea quickly overran South Korea around the border and began moving south on the peninsula.

Just two days after North Korea attacked, on June 27, President Rhee fled the capital city of Seoul. Shortly after he left, the South Korean Army—in an attempt to prevent the North Korean forces from reaching the capital—blew up the main bridge into and out of the city. This measure was unsuccessful; Seoul fell to the North Korean army on June 28. What was more, thousands of refugees were on the bridge when it was destroyed, resulting in hundreds of deaths and hundreds of more injuries.

Needless to say, this did nothing to endear the South Korean people to Rhee, his government, or his military. Many who may have otherwise taken his side or at least remained neutral undoubtedly sided with the North Korean communists, a fact that would make the fighting in the south more difficult. To make matters worse, Rhee ordered many political dissidents murdered as he fled the city. Certainly at least some of them were innocent, but they lost their lives nonetheless.

Over the coming days and weeks, North Koreans made further and further inroads into the southern portion of the peninsula at an alarming rate. By September, North Korean forces, aided by the Chinese, controlled almost the entire peninsula other than the very south-eastern tip. As they moved swiftly through the peninsula, individual South Korean troops as well as entire units defected and switched loyalties to the North Koreans, especially in light of the brutal way Rhee had fled the capital. By all measures, it looked like the North Koreans would achieve their goal of uniting the Korean peninsula under communist rule. However, the United States and the rest of the world did not sit idly by. Intervention was already in the works.

Chapter Four

The United States Enters the Korean War

"You are remembered for the rules you break."

—American General Douglas MacArthur

The United Nations was the first non-Korean player to take action in the wake of the initial invasion, and they did so swiftly. On the very day that the war broke out, the UN sanctioned North Korea and condemned their actions, clearly placing the blame with them. The Soviet Union objected to several aspects of the resolution, further escalating tensions.

Harry S. Truman was President of the United States when North Korea invaded South Korea, having become president in April 1945 when Franklin D. Roosevelt passed away during his unprecedented fourth term. It was toward the end of World War II, and Truman was thrust into the role of seeing the United States through the end of the conflict.

Roosevelt did not keep his vice president well-informed. Truman did not even know that the United States had been developing atomic weapons; he learned about them and had to decide whether to use them quickly. His decision to drop two atomic bombs on

Japanese cities not only shaped his legacy, but it also shaped Americans' expectations of Truman throughout the rest of his presidency.

While he was not originally elected to the office, he won a narrow victory against Republican nominee Thomas E. Dewey in the election of 1948; Americans thus put their trust in him to see them through the first years of the Cold War. The conflict in Korea was not the first foreign relations challenge that Truman faced, but it would be one of the biggest. One of the most important aspects of the Korean War would be Truman's decision *not* to use the United States' stores of nuclear weapons.

Truman was an ardent believer in Containment and the Domino Theory. When North Korea invaded South Korea, though, this was not the reason he (and other member nations of the United Nations) gave for intervening. Kim Il-sung was compared to Hitler; his aggressive invasion was compared to Hitler's aggression in the 1930s. Britain, the United States, and other allied nations appeased Hitler's aggressive moves, which became one of the factors they later recognized as causing the war. Therefore, it was easy to sell intervention in Korea to the American people by arguing that intervention in Korea would prevent the rise of another dictator like Hitler. Whether or not there was any truth to this argument, later in his life, Truman did admit that Containment was actually a primary cause of U.S. intervention in Korea. Congress appropriated funds, and the U.S. intervention in the war began.

The Hitler justification used to sway American public opinion was important. Just five years after the end of World War II, the world was still weary, and wary, of warfare. So much destruction had occurred, and much of the world was still struggling to rebuild. Not to mention, countless families around the world has lost loved ones, military personnel as well as civilians. To make matters even worse, everyone was fearful that because they were living in the "nuclear age," war inevitably meant the use of atomic weapons, whose horror was fresh in everyone's minds.

The "nuclear age" mindset had another impact on American involvement in the war. After the end of World War II, Truman's government had been steadily scaling back the size of the military. Fearful that the end of the war would see a return of the Great Depression, government spending turned to economic security. Cold War concerns also did not prompt the United States to maintain a large standing army: Instead, government spending concentrated on helping weak foreign nations rebuild (thus making them dependent on aid from the U.S. and less likely to turn to communism) and building up nuclear weapons, especially after the Soviet Union successfully detonated their first atomic bomb in 1949.

Nonetheless, patriotism and the memory of World War II also inspired a number of young American men to enlist in the military. They had been children, too young to actively participate in World War II, but had grown up watching the sacrifices of others. The Cold War was a time of ardent, almost militant patriotism in the country;

many therefore believed that they were doing their duty to protect their country.

It might be easy to assume that the might of the United States military would quickly crush the North Korean forces, but this was not the case. Truman's military cutbacks crippled initial efforts to push the North Koreans back toward the 38th parallel. They suffered relatively heavy losses in early engagements. What was more, when Truman ordered a naval blockade of North Korea, his military chiefs of staff had to inform him that because of his cutbacks, this was impossible. One of the lasting legacies of the Korean War would be that the United States, as well as some allies and other countries, realized the necessity of a large standing military. Never again would they be caught off guard during the Cold War.

As with involvement in any conflict, the Korean War was a heavily politicized event in the United States. By its end, it would have divided conservatives, who wanted the United States to be tougher on communism, and liberals, who were not completely convinced that actively pursuing communism was the correct course. In the wake of the Korean War, the United States would elect a former World War II commanding general – Dwight D. Eisenhower – as president. While he was a Republican, he was not ardently conservative, but his election still signaled what kind of leadership the American public desired.

Another famous World War II general would command the U.S. military in Korea: General Douglas

MacArthur. He was a hero of the war in the Pacific and a highly decorated officer. Truman did not jump into the war easily or quickly, though. He and General MacArthur disagreed from the beginning about how the war should be conducted, and their relationship would disintegrate over the course of the military campaign.

As Commander in Chief of the armed forces, Truman had the final say in how the United States conducted the war. His first priority was evacuating the U.S. citizens caught up in the fighting and in helping the armed forces of the Republic of Korea, rather than immediately committing his country's own troops. This was not the course of action favored by MacArthur.

As the United States and the United Nations prepared for war, the United States also engaged some troops in preventative positions. Namely, they stationed some naval ships in the waters around communist China.

It would be a few weeks before U.S. forced were engaged in anything but small skirmishes. On July 5, 1950, the Battle of Osan took place. A South Korean city located well to the south of the peninsula, south of Seoul, Osan and its location represented how far the North Korean troops had encroached into South Korea.

This battle was meant to be a preventative engagement. Since it happened relatively early in the U.S. involvement in the war, those involved in it were among the first U.S. troops to reach Korea. As the U.S. mobilized for a more fortified invasion, the goal of this particular force was just to prevent North Koreans from capturing more territory.

It did not go well for the Americans. Using Soviet artillery, North Korea quickly overran the out-gunned American units as Osan. After Soviet tanks had rolled through, the Americans regrouped, and were able to hold back the advancing infantry, but even this victory was short-lived. The North Korean infantry was eventually able to force back the American troops and move further south on the peninsula. The battle saw about 180 casualties between those killed, captured, and injured.

Even though it was relatively minor, the Battle of Osan had a major impact on the American involvement in the war. It showed how woefully unprepared the U.S. military was for war against Korea, or any other country for that matter. It was not just the army's equipment, either; the soldiers, and their leaders, were poorly trained and unprepared for battle.

Things would get worse for the Americans in Korea over the coming days, particularly for the 24th Infantry Division, which had fought at Osan. As the North Korean army marched southward, they defeated Americans at three more cities—Pyongtaek, Chonan, and then Chochiwon—over the next eight days. By July 14, the Eighth Army Division had lost more soldiers, and, much to the dismay of the South Koreans, the Americans, and all those who dreaded the Domino Theory, more territory.

Almost as soon as these engagements ended, the Americans were involved in yet another battle. After being forced further south once again, they gathered in the city of Taejon, establishing a headquarters, making it more vital to protect.

Chiefly, it was the 24th Division who was engaged in this battle, and they had already suffered many losses, not to mention fatigue from days of almost constant fighting. If they had not been prepared to fight before, they certainly were now.

At least initially, fighting took place chiefly along the banks of the Kum River. Nearly all of the members of the 24th Infantry Division took part. Over the course of several days, the out-manned, out-gunned, and out-trained Americans were unable to hold their position. They retreated into the city, where a fierce battle in the streets ensued. North Korea wanted to possess the city itself, after all, and thus their goal was to get rid of American troops and their headquarters entirely.

Fighting in the city only took place over the last two or three days of the battle, which lasted from July 14 to July 21. However, it was the fiercest and caused much destruction. While many civilians had fled during the fighting outside the actual city, many also still remained, and they suffered casualties.

The fighting between North Korean and American troops was often for the possession of small pieces of territories: businesses, parks, single structures, and even homes. This meant that much of the fighting was "up close and personal," and especially brutal. When the battle was over, Americans had suffered heavy losses (the reason they retreated from the city in the first place). More than two hundred men were injured, over nine hundred killed, and a staggering 2,400 missing. This was out of nearly three thousand total missing soldiers and about 3,600 casualties when the engagements following Osan were included.

What was more, the commander of the 24th Infantry Division, Major General William Dean, was badly injured and among the captured. He would be the highest-ranking soldier captured in the entire war. He was imprisoned in the North Korean city of Pyongyang until the end of the war. He was awarded the Medal of Honor—the U.S. military's highest commendation—for his part in the Battle of Taejon.

It was obvious to all that the war in Korea was going very badly for the Americans. It is not clear whether they expected a swift victory or not, but it quickly became evident that they were ill-prepared. This would become one of the biggest factors in the build-up of the American standing army over the coming decade; but first, the United States had a war to win, and since they so ardently believed in Containment and the Domino Theory, the safety of their own government and the governments of their allies also hung in the balance.

Chapter Five

The Korean War Escalates

"You know, North Korea's situation is far worse than East Germany, and South Korea is weaker than West Germany."

—Kim Dae Jung

Despite recognizing the obvious fact that the war was not going in its favor, America was not immediately able to turn things around. Over the course of the rest of July and the beginning weeks of August, North Korea made more and more progress southward, overrunning large swaths of the peninsula.

To make matters worse, both the Americans and the South Koreans were becoming more keenly aware of the urgency of the situation. As the fighting intensified, North Korea was cracking down on any opposition to their control. As they took more territory, they began investigating anyone they suspected of disloyalty to their new regime. Their veritable witch-hunt came to center on the educated and artistic; these people included teachers and professors as well as students, painters, and public intellectuals. Many of them were killed, along with others, almost indiscriminately.

American leadership, particularly General Douglas MacArthur, became very concerned with these turns of events. MacArthur even went so far as to issue statements—veiled threats—to Kim Il-sung about the killings. However, there was little else he or anyone could do until the military was able to successfully retaliate, stop the North Korean southward movement, and push them back up into their own territory. As the weeks went on, the war became more of a humanitarian effort, with atrocities committed on both sides.

The next major engagement began at the beginning of August and lasted through mid-September. The Battle of Pusan Perimeter, as it came to be known, allowed the United Nations forces (of which the U.S. was a part, for this engagement) to keep their mission in Korea alive.

As is by now obvious, North Korea was winning the war through attrition. With little resistance, they made their way through the peninsula. The United Nations and U.S. forces were forced all the way back to Pusan (today known as Busan), a city on the south-eastern coast, surrounded on most sides by the Sea of Japan, rivers, and mountains. Its terrain made it more difficult to access for the enemy, but since the UN forces had ample time (they began falling back to the position in July), they were able to fortify about a 140 mile stretch in and around the city before North Korean troops arrived in August.

Pusan was also important because it was a port city. The United Nations and American forces used it not only to land new troops for the war but also the supplies needed to sustain those troops: everything from food to ammunition, to clothing, to letters from home. Even though the North Koreans would not have completely overrun the peninsula had Pusan fallen, the war would have been essentially lost for the south. Holding the port was key to staying alive for the forces supporting South Korea.

Because the United Nations forces had stretched themselves around such a large perimeter, North Korea had a lot of options about how to launch an offensive. They could attack at four possible points, each with distinct terrain, advantages, and disadvantages. Perhaps emboldened by their recent victories against United States forces in their march southward, the North Korean military leadership decided to split their forces into four divisions and attack each of the United Nations strongholds. By doing so, they hoped to bring about a swift victory and move on quickly. However, they underestimated the strength of the U.N. and American forces as well as their fortifications. The Battle of Pusan lasted more than a month, as prolonged fighting went on in several different locations. Most notably, the fighting took place at Taegu (where carpet bombing was also conducted by the U.S.), Naktong Bulge, and P'ohang-dong.

This was a fatal mistake on the part of the North Koreans and began to turn the tide of the war. Their divided forces had trouble not only communicating with one another, but also with supplies. The division of their forces did not result in swift victory; quite to the contrary, it slowed it down, which gave the U.N. time to make use of its vast resources.

The Soviet Union obviously supported communist North Korea as it moved southward, but their support could not be too overt, nor could it be too obvious, given the nuclear tensions existing between it and the United States. Because the Soviet Union could not fully commit its air support, the United Nations had a clear advantage here. During the weeks that the Battle of Pusan dragged on, the UN was able to cut into North Korean supply lines more and more using air power. The Chinese could not aid the North Koreans very much in this arena either, as their capabilities to offer support were largely on the ground.

As the weeks went on to the end of the battle on September 15, North Korea's troops were becoming more and more haggard. They were running out of food and clothing. They were tired because replacement soldiers could not reach them, either to relieve those still fighting or replace those who had been killed. Also, they were afraid, as their supply of ammunition and functioning weaponry was diminishing.

Air coverage played a major role in this battle. In fact, air superiority during this battle would impact the rest of the war. While so many North Korean troops were engaged at Pusan, the United States Air Force, in particular, launched daily offenses. They strategically destroyed infrastructure that would have facilitated North Korean troop and supply movements. They also destroyed depots and fuel repositories used by North Koreans. They sought out the troops themselves, so much so that North Korean forces had no choice but to move only at night.

The Battle of Pusan very much allowed the United States and United Nations forces to catch their breath, but it knocked the wind out of the North Koreans.

However, all of this is not to say that the United Nations forces were faring substantially better. Although they were more able to resupply their troops (they did so by sea, sending what was needed from U.S. bases in nearby Japan), they, too were suffering due to the length and nature of the fighting. In fact, throughout much of the battle, the two sides were deadlocked along the perimeter established by the United Nations. In September, though, they were confident that they had the upper hand since their forces numbered almost twice those of the Korean People's Army. They launched a successful counteroffensive, pushing the North Koreans north, and the tide of the war changed. It was not without staggering cost, though. In fact, the entire battle was bloody on both sides; everyone suffered very high numbers of casualties. About 4,600 American soldiers were killed and 12,000 wounded, though this number pales in comparison to South Korea's 40,000 casualties.

After the Battle of Pusan, the stage was set for the September 1950 Battle of Inchon, one of the most well-remembered and consequential battles of the war. The location was not the most obvious choice for the battle, though, because it was well behind North Korean lines (more than 150 kilometers) and into the territory they had already captured.

But the location was strategic. In fact, General MacArthur wanted to land troops at Inchon (now

Incheon) from the beginning of the war. However, he met opposition from other generals and strategists back in Washington, D.C. It was probably good that he was not able to land at Inchon sooner, though: The Battle of Pusan had weakened North Korean forces enough that the amphibious landing was much less difficult.

Even though the Korean People's Army had been severely weakened, this did not mean that the Battle of Inchon was painless or quick. On the contrary, the battle caused great death and destruction among civilians and infrastructure.

The landing was massive. Called Operation Chromite, it involved 75,000 United Nations troops, many of them American, commanded by General MacArthur. They landed on September 15th, while the Battle of Pusan was still ongoing (it would end on September 18). At the same time as the surprise amphibious attack began, U.N. forces also began providing air support by bombing strategic locations around the city.

Largely because of the Battle of Pusan, Inchon was poorly defended; the North Koreans had very few troops there. Some began moving back toward Inchon immediately (which helped end the Battle of Pusan), but they were tired and weary from battle.

The UN forces depended on the fact that Inchon was poorly defended and that there were few North Korean troops in the area. This meant that keeping the battle a secret was of paramount importance to its success (hence why it had a code name in the first place). Even some of the troops themselves did not know where they were headed or what they were training for during the time they spent in Japan.

As the date of the invasion approached, the United Nations became aware of a new threat. Using equipment provided by the Soviet Union, the North Koreans had placed naval mines all along the Korean coastline in order to prevent the very kind of attack that they did not know was being planned. There was no way for the United Nations forces to try to locate or detonate these naval mines around Inchon before the invasion, as that would have given away the location; again, surprise was of the utmost importance.

However, the location proved to be strategic for this reason as well, and it only increased General MacArthur's reputation and ego. There were very few naval mines placed near Inchon, for the plain reason that North Korea did not believe Inchon was of great enough importance (strategic or otherwise) and did not anticipate an invasion here.

Needless to say, the surprise was successful. The troops landed at three places on September 15: Green Beach early in the morning, Red Beach in the afternoon, and much later (after the North Koreans had retreated), Blue Beach. The Battle of Inchon was relatively quick, especially in comparison to the Battle of Pusan, largely because troops and artillery needed to be re-routed to Inchon (at the urging of Stalin and the Soviet Union; Kim Il-sung did not take this initiative or make this decision until the Soviets intervened). As a result, the Battle of

Pusan ended on September 18, and the Battle of Inchon on September 19.

These combined victories were important on many levels. It stopped North Korea's advance and ended their "winning streak," it gave the battle-weary South Korean military a break, and, perhaps most importantly, it gave the people of South Korea hope after watching their homes and their friends fall victim to the invading North.

The victory at Inchon also allowed the United Nations forces, under the command of General MacArthur, to recapture Seoul, the South Korean capital. This happened less than a week after the Battle of Inchon ended, on September 25. Pusan and Inchon allowed the troops to make this advance, but at the same time, once again, superior air power also made a difference. The air forces used massive strategic bombing to cripple North Korea's artillery holdings.

None of this meant that capturing Seoul was easy, however. In the process of making their way to Seoul, the United Nations faced some opposition; however, when they reached the city, they found it heavily fortified and relatively well defended. Bitter fighting ensued as the forces, mostly United States Marines, captured the city painfully slowly. The fighting moved from building to building until the Marines were finally able to capture the important government buildings that signified victory.

Part of the brutal nature of the fighting resulted from the fact that the U.S. commander, General Edward Almond, desperately wanted to capture the city by September 25. The date had symbolic significance: it marked three months, to the day, that North Korea had crossed the 38th parallel and the war had officially begun. Perhaps the severity and the brutality of the battle was a result of this hurry, or perhaps it was inevitable, given the importance of Seoul and the tensions existing between the two sides. Either way, the battle was not without atrocities. On September 26, as both sides fought over control of a hotel, the U.S. Marines took several North Korean prisoners. Later eye-witness accounts reported that twelve of these prisoners were disarmed, stripped, and executed in the hotel basement.

Even worse were the Goyang Geumjeong Cave Massacre and the Namyangju Massacre, both aimed to destroy whatever communist and North Korean sympathies remained in or around the city. Even though General Almond declared victory on September 25, fighting continued, as the city was not really secured, especially in outlying areas. In the Goyang Geumjeong Cave Massacre, at least 153 civilians were killed by South Korean police and military forces between October 9 and the 31st. Later investigations revealed that eight minors and seven women were among those killed, and it was also revealed that the vast majority of the victims were not related to North Koreans or South Korean rebels.

The Namyangju Massacre had the same goal: to destroy North Korea's hold on the south. It was even bigger and more brutal. It lasted from October 1950 through early 1951 and involved more than 450 deaths. More than twenty of the victims were young children under ten years old. Later investigations yielded the same outcome: evidence that the victims had connections to communists or North Koreans did not exist.

It should be noted that actions such as these are common during all wars. It would be difficult to search the historical annals and find any war that was fought without atrocities on either side. However, it is also important to note that these methods are almost always counter-productive. While torture and mass murder may work to quell unrest in the short term, in the end, those who survive are frequently unsympathetic to those who perpetrated the atrocities, as well as their allies. In this case, it is not hard to see that the South Koreans who watched their innocent friends, neighbors, and even family members rounded up and massacred would harbor deep mistrust and resentment toward the South Korean government, the United States, and the United Nations. Despite the fact that this pattern has been repeated again and again in history, these kinds of devastating events continue to happen.

The recapture of Seoul was important for several reasons: it restored some semblance of order to South Korea by regaining its seat of government. It also boosted morale among South Koreans, military and civilian alike (though not those touched by the brutal massacres that came with it). It cut off important supply lines that the North Korean Army depended on after their supply lines were already stretched very thin. Also, it gave the United Nations and South Korean forces a strategic air base. Prior to the capture, they had been primarily using

Japanese bases. Now, the air support they were able to provide would be much more effective.

Just as the United States celebrated the victories of the United Nations forces, Stalin and Soviet leadership were frustrated and furious, mostly at the incompetence of the North Korean military. The Chinese military leaders who had been sent by Stalin to aid North Korea had advised Kim Il-sung against trying to defend Inchon in the first place; obviously, he ignored them. In response, in a move that endangered his country's anonymity in the war, Stalin called an emergency meeting of the Politburo, the political party that ran the Soviet Union. While he condemned the actions of the North Korean leadership, he also blamed his own military leaders for the failure; they were supposed to be controlling the war via the Chinese.

It is not unreasonable to call the Battle of Pusan, the Battle of Inchon, and the subsequent capture of Seoul the turning point in the war. The North Korean southerly advance was stopped. They lost control of much of the territory they had gained in their initial push. Their ability to supply their military was diminished. Also, their ability to continue fighting was severely limited: they had lost a significant number of troops and a very significant percentage of their artillery, ammunition, and other supplies.

For the South Koreans, the United Nations forces, and the U.S. forces, the opposite was the case. Morale was higher, and they were better protected and supplied than ever before. However, this is not to say that the rest of the war would be easy, or that it would be quick. Several more years of fighting ensued, and in the end, many people all over the world wondered what the war—and all its death and destruction—had been for in the first place.

Chapter Six

Stalemate at the 38ᵗʰ Parallel

"Of the nations of the world, Korea alone, up to now, is the sole one which has risked its all against communism. The magnificence of the courage and fortitude of the Korean people defies description."

—General Douglas MacArthur

The Korean War was a war of attrition: both sides marked victory by gaining or maintaining territory. Therefore, after the victories at Inchon and Seoul, it was imperative that the UN forces keep pushing. Thus began the UN Offensive in the Korean War.

A strategic question loomed over United States leadership: whether or not to pursue the North Koreans north of the 38ᵗʰ parallel, the line that had divided North and South Korea, and the line the North Koreans crossed when they started the war. A major concern was whether crossing this line would prompt the Soviet Union or the Chinese to intervene; the United States did not want a long, protracted war with another major world power. Truman authorized MacArthur to cross, but only if there was no presence of other powers in Korea.

Just three days after issuing that warning to MacArthur, on September 30, Truman's Secretary of Defense, George Marshall, authorized MacArthur to pursue the North Koreans back into their own territory. The very next day, MacArthur crossed the 38th parallel.

In response, on October 1, the Chinese officially entered the war. They did so in response to what they perceived as aggression on the part of the United States and the United Nations. They also did so in response to appeals from Kim Il-sung, and with permission from Stalin, though not without resistance from some Chinese leaders. Nonetheless, the Chinese entered the war officially on October 8. Troops arrived in Korea on October 25, after the Chinese had secured a commitment from Stalin that he would send some supplies to support the offensive.

Fighting thus continued between the United States/United Nations/South Koreans and North Koreans and Chinese. That it continued to be a war of attrition meant that the goal of the battles was capturing cities and more terrain.

The Chinese army was very well-trained and well-disciplined. The UN forces were not even sure that they had intervened in the war: they moved only at night and were very well camouflaged. Later, after the Chinese had engaged UN forces and quickly retreated, UN and U.S. leadership wondered whether they had left the war. They had not, however. The two sides were fairly well matched, which meant that the war was starting to drag out, despite the United States' and MacArthur's "Home by Christmas" offensive and the resulting Battle of the Ch'ongch'on River, which began on November 25 and lasted until

December 2 in north-western North Korea (near the Chinese border).

This battle was primarily between the Chinese 13th Army and the United States Eighth Army. Chinese strategic positions caused very heavy losses on U.S. and United Nations forces, forcing a retreat; this time, the Chinese gave chase back to the 38th parallel. The Eighth Army's forces were so badly weakened that other U.S. and UN divisions fighting in North Korea were also forced to retreat in order to reinforce them.

Then began the Hungnam Evacuation of the UN forces. Soldiers, as well as supplies, were evacuated en masse from Hungnam, a port city on the eastern shore of North Korea. They were taken back to Pusan, a strategic location that was also symbolic: it was at Pusan that they had first turned the tide of the war and been able to chase North Koreans back over the border.

The war degenerated from there, not only for the United Nations and the United States forces but also for the Chinese (who mostly took over the fighting from this point on). Fighting continued, mostly around the 38th parallel, for several months. For South Korea, their priority was expelling all North Korean sympathizers and communists within their borders. More atrocities were carried out—the Geochang Massacre and Sancheong-Hamyang Massacre. In the Geochang Massacre, more than seven hundred people were killed, more than half of them children. More than seven hundred were killed at Sancheong-Hamyang as well, and most of them were women, children, and elderly.

Internal issues also plagued United States leadership, most poignantly the relationship between Truman, the American president and Commander in Chief of the armed forces, and General MacArthur, who was commanding U.S. and UN forces in Korea. MacArthur refused to fly back to the United States to meet with Truman late in 1950, forcing Truman to come to the Pacific. MacArthur often refused to communicate.

Truman blamed MacArthur for the turn the war had taken. Truman had warned MacArthur against crossing the 38th parallel if the Chinese or Soviets were likely to intervene. Truman believed MacArthur had ignored obvious warnings from the Chinese that they would intervene and recklessly crossed the 38 th parallel anyway, prompting them to enter the war and causing many U.S. deaths.

To make matters between Truman and MacArthur even worse, MacArthur ardently believed that, as the military commander, he had the authority to use nuclear weapons. He seriously considered using atomic weapons against the North Koreans and Chinese in order to interrupt their supply lines and weaken their ability to fight. Truman—as President and Commander in Chief—disagreed; he believed only he had the authority to launch America's nuclear stores. On top of that, he feared that MacArthur would act recklessly and initiate a nuclear war with the Soviet Union.

Finally, MacArthur and Truman disagreed about the goals and outcomes of the war. MacArthur was an all-or-nothing general. He did not believe that the U.S. could declare victory without annihilating the North Korean threat, by fighting until North Korea surrendered unconditionally and communism could be eliminated on the peninsula. Truman, on the other hand, had a more circumspect view of America's role in the war. He believed that America was in Korea to maintain peace, not to initiate regime change. If the division between North and South Korea was to be protected at the 38th parallel, the United States had achieved what it set out to do.

The conflict between the Commander in Chief and the military commander grew worse and worse. In the end, President Truman fired General Douglas MacArthur. This was an especially dramatic and symbolic event, as these two men had both been instrumental in winning World War II for the allies. Now, less than a decade later, they seemed to be enemies.

What was more, their division exemplified the polarized nature of American politics and society at the time. What were the U.S. goals in the Cold War? According to the policy of Containment, preventing the spread of communism was of the utmost importance. But should the U.S. be more active in rooting out and eliminating communism where it already existed, rather than just containing it? Clearly, MacArthur believed this was so while Truman disagreed in this case. When MacArthur returned to the United States, he made an address before Congress in which he laid out his beliefs about the dangers of communism and what America's goals in the Cold War should be. It represented the polarized views of Americans throughout the country.

Meanwhile, the war continued in Korea. Whether or not the war remained one of attrition, neither side was able to gain much ground. The fighting largely took place around the 38th parallel. About ten actual battles took place during the rest of 1951, 1952, and through July of 1953. The fighting was mostly between American and Chinese troops; neither North nor South Korea was able to provide much participation.

It became clear that the war had stalemated. Therefore, armistice negotiations commenced in July 1953. The major point of contention was not the cessation of fighting or even where Korea would be divided; the biggest conflict was the release of prisoners of war.

Finally, in 1954, an armistice was signed. In the end, the war in Korea did not result in any territorial change. The border between North Korea and South Korea remained at the 38th parallel. North Korea remained communist and controlled by a dictatorship, and the South Korean economy was capitalistic, with an ostensibly republican government. A demilitarized zone was established along the 38th parallel, which would be protected and overseen by an international coalition. That demilitarized zone still exists today.

Chapter Eight

After the War

"Today, the Korean peninsula provides the world's clearest contract between a society that is open and a society that is closed; between a nation that is dynamic and growing, and a government that would rather starve its people than change. It's a contrast so stark you can see it from space, as the brilliant lights of Seoul give way to the utter darkness in the north."

—United States President Barack Obama, 2010

Today, North and South Korea are still divided along the 38th parallel. North Korea is still communist and is now ruled by Kim Il-sung's grandson, Kim Jong-un after his father Kim Jong-il passed away. South Korea is an ally of the United States and other western countries.

North Korea is frequently in the news. Even after the end of the Cold War, the United States did not ease relations with its chief communist rivals, especially Cuba and North Korea. To this day, North Korea remains on extremely unfriendly terms with the United States and allies of the U.S. as well.

North Korea maintains a very strong standing army and spends a great deal of money on weapons. Chief among its goals is becoming a nuclear power, capable of fighting a nuclear war against the United States and other nations. This is worrisome to many around the world who consider Kim Jong-un to be an unstable leader.

Since North Korea isolates itself from relations with most of the rest of the world, it is difficult to know for sure what life is like inside its borders. However, it is fairly certain that many North Koreans are suffering. For one thing, they live in a repressive regime without the ability to speak their minds. If they do, they risk reprisal by the government. What is more, the North Korean economy is not strong, and many North Koreans do not have enough to eat and lack sufficient clothing, shelter, and medical care, the basic necessities of life. Kim Jong-un and representatives of his government deny these conditions exist.

South Korea stands in sharp contrast to its northern neighbor, its brother, and its enemy. While North Korea is focused on military build-up and struggles to feed its people, South Korea is a full-fledged capitalist economy. Its primary goals center on technology and industry. It is a very urban country as well. The city of Seoul is crowded and has grown exponentially over the years. However, South Korea also has its share of issues, including poverty and abusive labor practices.

Obviously, the impact of the Korean War was most deeply felt by the Korean people. However, just as it had worldwide causes and implications, it also had worldwide repercussions. One of the most important outcomes of the Korean War was something that did *not* happen: no atomic weapons were used by either side in the war. The dropping of atomic weapons on Japan in order to end

World War II caused unprecedented, horrific destruction and death that shocked the world. Once the Soviet Union successfully detonated the first atomic weapons of their own, the United States, the Soviet Union, and the entire world feared that warfare would always involve the use of these weapons of mass destruction. How could they know that the very nature of warfare had not evolved before their eyes?

By not using their growing stores of atomic weapons, both sides in the Cold War demonstrated that war did not need to devolve in such a way. In fact, one of the outcomes of the Korean War might even be that it made the world *more* safe for more war by demonstrating that all-out destruction need not be the automatic result. It certainly changed the course of the Cold War. However, perhaps the great irony of the Korean War is that now, North Korea stands poised to plunge the world into nuclear war.

Conclusion

How should we categorize, and understand, the Korean War? It was not exactly a civil war, but neither was it a war between two foreign combatants. It was a quintessential Cold War event, and while it is easy to analyze it from that perspective, it is also important to keep in mind the impact it has had on Asia and on the Korean people.

Even though the war was relatively unpopular at the time, and even though American casualties remained low in comparison to the wars on either end of it (World War II and the Vietnam War), *and* even though the purpose of the war was so wrapped up in Cold War politics, the United States has erected a haunting memorial to it in Washington, D.C. Located on the National Mall near the Lincoln Memorial, Washington Monument, and Vietnam War Memorial, it consists of nineteen impressively detailed steel statues of soldiers fighting the war. Just as impressive, on the side of the memorial is a mural wall, which incorporates over 2,500 actual etched photos of the American and UN efforts in the war. It is a haunting reminder.

Washington, D.C. is not the only place that Americans have established a memorial to the war. A monument was erected at the site of the Battle of Osan, the first engagement involving Americans in the Korean War. Since the U.S. military still uses a nearby site as a station, it holds an annual commemoration of the battle on July 5, its anniversary.

One wonders whether North and South Korea will ever be able to unite. The two nations on the Korean peninsula share a common history that stretches back several millennia. However, the longer they remain divided by the 38th parallel, the more they grow apart.

[1] The Jeju uprising continues to be a controversial event to this day, especially since tensions surrounding communism in Korea are still high. Many families do not have answers about what happened to their loved ones, and the atrocities committed on both sides have not been fully investigated.

Made in the USA
Lexington, KY
01 May 2017